Money Matters for

S0-AFI-217

Text and Illustrations ©1997 by Lauree and L. Allen Burkett

Money Matters for Kids
Executive Producers Lauree and L. Allen Burkett
Written by Lauree Burkett and Christie Bowler
Illustrated by Chris Kielesinski, Illustrations Inked by Ken Save
Puzzles Illustrated by Ed Strauss

For Lightwave Publishing
Managing Editor: Elaine Osborne
Project Assistant: Ed Strauss
Text Director: Christie Bowler
Design: Terry VanRoon
Desktop Publishing: Andrew Jaster

All rights reserved. No part of this book may be reproduced in any form without permission in writing from the publisher, except in the case of brief quotations embodied in critical articles or reviews.

All Scripture quotations, unless indicated, are taken from the Holy Bible: New International Version®. Copyright © 1973, 1978, 1984 by International Bible Society. Used by permission of Zondervan Publishing House. All rights reserved.

The "NIV" and "New International Version" trademarks are registered in the United States Patent and Trademark Office by International Bible Society. Use of either trademark requires permission of International Bible Society.

ISBN: 0-8024-6343-6

1 3 5 7 9 10 8 6 4 2

Printed in the United States of America

Money Matters for KIDS

a Lauree and L. Allen Burkett Presentation

Written by
Lauree Burkett
Christie Bowler

Illustrated by **Chris Kielesinski**

MOODY PRESS
CHICAGO

CONTENTS

WELCOME TO MONEY MATTERS!

Welcome to what matters, kids! You're in for the learning time of your lives! We've got superheros, slides, golden eggs, and treasure maps! We've got puzzles, jokes, trivia, and challenges.

WAIT! Before you turn the page, you need to know a few things about money—such as what it is. Any ideas? Naw, it's not just pieces of paper or little bits of metal. If it's just paper, why won't the corner store take any bit of paper you hand over in exchange for candy? What's so special about the particular paper and metal we call money?

We all know what money is and what it isn't. The government, banks, store owners, and everyone in the country agree that particular papers and certain bits of metal have special value. Money, standard pieces of metal and paper stamped by the government, is used as a medium of exchange—we exchange the money for something of equal value, such as candy.

Say you deliver newspapers and want candy. The corner store has candy but doesn't need newspapers delivered. You need something the store wants to exchange for candy. Money! The store owner tells you how much the candy is worth. You take your pay for delivering newspapers and exchange it for the candy.

One more thing. You'll find that learning about money isn't just about paper and metal and how we use it. Nope. It's about our attitudes toward money, what we do with it and why, whether we let it control our lives, and how well we manage it. It's about recognizing it all belongs to God. He's loaned it to us to use for His glory.

Money can be a monster! Give it a little control—it wants it all. Get a little—it tries to make you want more. You think more money will make you happy, so you work hard and get more. But you're still unhappy—you have to have MORE! It can be a dangerous beast. You have to teach it who's boss. That's exactly what this book will teach you. Ready? OK, turn the page and hang on for the adventure!

INSTRUCTIONS FOR TREASURE HUNTS

Hey kids! In each of the Treasure Hunt sections there is a great game. Take the first letter of each of the words printed in green and then unscramble them to find a piece of the armor of God (found in Ephesians 6:14–17) or one or two of the fruits of the Spirit (found in Galatians 5:22,23). Here's the list of the things you will find:

Belt of Truth
Armor of Godliness
Shoes of Good News
Shield of Faith
Helmet of Salvation
Sword of God's Word

Patience
Love
Kindness
Peace
Goodness
Joy
Faithfulness
Gentleness
Self-Control

Have fun finding them!

STEWARD-SHIP

Larry the Cat

Imagine you have a pet you really love. If you go away for a month, who will look after it? You'll probably ask a friend that you trust to watch over your pet. You know you can count on your friend to take good care of it.

God has done just that! He's given some of His valuable possessions to be taken care of by His friends. Who are His friends? All of us who've asked Jesus to take away our sins and come live in our hearts. When we've done that we belong to Him and Jesus says we're His friends. (If you haven't asked Jesus to come into your heart, ask your parents or pastor for help or contact the publisher. You'll find the address in the back of this book.) Being Jesus' friends makes us God's friends, too. God's given us, His friends, all kinds of things to look after—everything we have, in fact.

Think about it. What do you have that you didn't receive? The Apostle Paul asked the same question. *"For who makes you different from anyone else? What do you have that you did not receive? And if you did receive it, why do you boast as though you did not?"* (1 Corinthians 4:7)

If you think carefully, you'll see that everything came from somewhere else. And, if you trace back as far as you can go, you'll find it all came from God—money, possessions, time, energy, abilities, etc. All these things are really God's. He's loaned them to us and made us responsible to care for them and use them wisely. We're managing God's stuff for Him. The Bible calls that being His "stewards."

To be a good steward, we first need to understand that all the things and abilities we're managing aren't ours. They don't belong to us. They're God's. They're just on loan. Then we need to commit ourselves to managing and using them the way the owner (God) wants us to.

Don't worry. God loves us. He knows what's best for us. You'll find that doing what God wants, and doing things His way, works out great! That's the reason He wants us to do it His way—He wants us to have His best.

Read Matthew 25:14–30.

JOKE:

Do rabbits use combs?
No, they use harebrushes.

A STEWARD'S HOUSE RULES

HOUSE RULES

"I'm HO-OME!" you yell, racing in the door. You dump your schoolbooks, kick your shoes off, drop your coat, and open the fridge. You drink straight from the juice jug, then toss it in the sink. It breaks. Oops. You race into the family room, jump onto the couch, do a somersault, and kick the TV. It crashes to the floor. Glass flies everywhere. You race upstairs, knocking over vases and pictures. What a homecoming!

Would you do that? NOT! Why not? True, you'd get in big trouble. But think about it. The stuff you broke isn't yours. The house and everything in it belongs to your parents. They let you use their things, like the TV, VCR, fridge, and furniture. But they expect you to take care of it. You probably have house rules like "Don't jump on the furniture." Some things are just common sense—no grilled cheese sandwiches in the VCR.

Your parents own the house and its contents. They let you use it. But they expect you to take care of it. In that way, you're stewards of your parents' stuff—especially when they're out or you have friends over. In a small way that's like God and us. God's the ultimate owner of everything (yup, even your parents' house). God lets us use His stuff. We're His stewards. He expects us to treat His things wisely and take care of them. His "house rules" are written in the Bible.

Let's take a look at what we are stewards of.

THE STEWARD LIST

Ever heard of an acrostic? You put words in lines so certain letters, like the first of each line, spell out a word. The acrostic can teach us about the word it spells. Take "Steward." Each letter can stand for something we're stewards of.

Selves:

We're the "temple of God" because God's Spirit lives in us. That means we need to take care of our bodies, make sure we get enough food, rest, and exercise, and keep ourselves clean and nicely dressed. We also need to keep our minds and spirits clean and healthy by feeding them good thoughts, pictures, and ideas.

Time:

We can never get time back once it's gone, so we should make every minute count. That means using time wisely and not procras-tinating—putting stuff off (like homework and chores) until we run out of time. It's much better to do those things first. Then we'll have time to really enjoy ourselves, with no nagging

TRIVIA:

Before people used coins and paper for money, they used other things. In China, rice and small tools were used as money, while people in India used cowry shells and Hong Kong citizens used gambling counters.

God made you just as you are — you are unique! He has great plans for your life.

feeling that we should be studying or working. It also means giving our lives to God and spending each moment, day, week, month, and year as He wants us to.

Everything:

This means all we own—our treasures, possessions, and money. That's easy to understand. Everything we have ultimately comes from God. It's our responsibility to look after it for Him and use it wisely. God loves us to have fun so it's our job to enjoy what He's given us. That sounds easy! Just remember, because it's God's we should be ready, willing, and eager to share it with others.

JOKE:
Why did the dalmatian refuse to bathe in the dishwasher detergent?
He didn't want to come out spotless.

Will:

You have choices you have to make. This is called using your will. The choices you make are your responsibility. The most important choice you must make is whether you'll do things your way (self will) or God's way.

Abilities:

What kinds of things are you good at? What do you like doing better than anything else? Do you know why this is? God gives each of us unique talents, abilities, and gifts. He designed you for a special purpose–and when you can count on God's power to use those gifts, you'll be filled with joy in whatever you do.

Relationships:

Other people are important in our lives—like friends, family and classmates. We should focus on others and their needs instead of ourselves. When we remember that the relationship is more important than the little details (who sat next to whom, who got invited first . . . you know what I mean), then we'll be the kind of friend we'd love to have.

Devotion to God:

We need to work on our relationship with God. He's our best friend. We trust Him with everything. We get to know Him and learn more about Him through the Bible, prayer, spending time with Him every day, and giving Him our lives and hearts. We do things His way because we know He loves us and always wants what's best for us.

GOD'S HOUSE RULES

OK, we're stewards, but how do we do it? Remember God's "house rules"? We check the Bible for the relevant rule. Here's the main one: *"Each one should use whatever gift he has received to serve others, faithfully administering God's grace in its various forms"* (1 Peter 4:10). This means our first thought is about how we can use something to help or serve someone else. It means looking after others before worrying about how we can benefit or have something.

Sometimes we can't figure out what to do. That's OK. God says if we ask for wisdom He'll give it to us (James 1:5). God's interested in our decisions. He wants us to make the best ones, so He'll help us figure them out. For example, the Bible has lots of instructions about money: we should tithe (Proverbs 3:9–10; Matthew 23:23), be ready to give to help people (Luke 6:31,38), not store it up as if it will take care of us (Matthew 6:19–21), always pay our debts (Psalm 37:21).

Stewardship is about our whole lives. Money can help us learn about stewardship because how we handle it can carry over into how we handle other areas of our lives. We should give our money, our time, and ourselves willingly. Money is a great, in-your-face, see-it-every-day reminder that we're stewards. So let your good money stewardship lead to good stewardship in the rest of your life.

IS THAT IT?

No way! That's just the beginning! Being good stewards is a two-way street.

Put ten pennies on a piece of paper, and write the words "God" and "Me" as shown. Now by moving only three pennies, make your money triangle point to "God" instead of yourself.

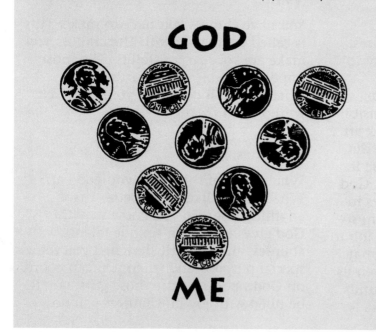

GOD

ME

What do you have that you did not receive? Use your gifts to serve others.

In fact, it's a superhighway coming our way! It's the best way to live. Why? It boils down to God's love.

Think about this: Why is sticking a grilled cheese sandwich in a VCR a bad idea? The VCR just won't work with cheese all over its innards. Why can't you punch holes in the walls or jump on furniture? Well, holes are ugly, and so is jumped on, trashed furniture (it's uncomfortable, too). And a trashed house won't sell very well—your parents would lose money, big time. But the main reason is that your parents are training you to be responsible. They know one day you'll have to look after a house, fix walls, buy furniture, and pay bills (like a mortgage). They want you to learn the skills and attitudes you'll need now so you'll have them later and have a better life. They train you because they love you.

Now think of God's love! He loves you way more than your parents love you. When God tells you to do things a certain way, you know He has a good reason. His reason is to give you a great life. He's training you to be the kind of person who'll have great friends, a good reputation, success in work, and peace and joy.

So go to the Steward's Instruction Manual and House Rule Book—the Bible—for help in knowing how to be God's stewards. Happy stewarding! It leads to the best life!

TRIVIA:

What do franc, mark, rupee, ringgitt, won, baht, and kwacha have in common? They're all money. Franc is French. Mark is German. Rupee is Indian. Ringgitt is Malaysian. Won is South Korean. Baht is from Thailand. And Kwacha is from Malawi.

TREASURE HUNT
MEMORY VERSE

1 Peter 4:10 —*Each one should use whatever gift he has received to serve others, faithfully administering God's grace in its various forms.*

BIBLE STUDY PASSAGE

Matthew 25:14–28; Romans 12:6–8 (Paraphrased)

Jesus told His disciples a story to explain what His kingdom is like. He said a man going on a journey called in three servants. He gave each an amount of money he knew they could take care of. Two used their money wisely and doubled it. But the man with the least was afraid of the master and did not trust him. He buried his money in a hole.

When the master returned, he said to the first two, *"²¹Well done, good and faithful servant! You've been faithful with a few things; I'll put you in charge of many things. Come and share your master's happiness!"* But to the one who hid his money, he said, *²⁶"You wicked, lazy servant! . . . ²⁷You should have put my money on deposit with* the bankers, so that when I returned I would have received *it back with interest. ²⁸Take the [money] from him."*

The apostle Paul says, *⁶"We have different gifts, according to the grace given us."* We should each cheerfully use the gifts God's given us according to His plan.

God created you. He's the one who truly owns everything you have. He has a plan for you. He wants you to be a good steward of all the gifts He's given you.

1. How did the master decide how much to give each servant?

2. What reward did the master give the servants who used the gifts (money in this story) he gave them?

3. It's easy to trust God when we get to know Him because we're sure He loves us and wants our best. What did the last servant's fear cause him to do?

Is there one thing in your life you're having a hard time using for God? Maybe a special talent, the kind of clothes you wear, or even how you spend your money? Ask God to help you use it for His glory.

TRUSTING GOD

Larry the Cat

Today's the day! Your grandparents have promised to take you out. You get to choose where you eat, and they'll buy you one present of your choice.

Oh, no! They're late! But you don't panic. You don't worry, because you trust your grandparents to do what they say. They love you, so you know they'll come.

God is like that. He's made promises, too. And He always keeps His promises. We can totally trust Him. His promises are written in the Bible along with instructions on how to do things. He's given us wisdom and principles to follow, and He promises to provide for us.

The Bible says, *"Give, and it will be given to you"* (Luke 6:38). We know that God's way is best because He's wise and He loves us. So we can give without worrying because we know God is looking after us and taking care of our needs. He's trustworthy. He loves us and knows what is best for us. He tells us to do things a certain way because that will give us the best lives.

This applies to our money and everything else. God understands money and knows how it works. We can trust that His way of dealing with money is the best way. God knows what we need and want. He knows how much money we have. We can ask Him for wisdom in using our money, and we can trust Him—no matter what. Remember, we also need to trust God when it comes to how much money He gives us. It's just enough! He may help us to be wiser in how we use our money instead of giving us more.

Since God knows how everything works best, we know life will be better when we trust Him and follow His instructions. When it doesn't look like God's way of doing things is working, that's when we really need to trust Him. He's working things out. Guaranteed!

You can count on God even more than you count on your grandparents!

JOKE:

What did the tree say to the woodchopper?
Leaf me alone.

Larry the Cat

LEARN THE TRUST TROT

THE TRUST THING

"Jump! I'll catch you. Trust me!" You peer down at the person in the water miles below the diving board. You can't quite see him, but he said he would catch you. Sure, you'll jump. Why not?

WAIT! Fine words do not trust make. You need to ask some questions first. Who is this person? Is he trustworthy? Why would he catch you? These are all good questions. Here's another. What are you doing up there in the first place? (Oh, the board's only two feet above the water, but you have a good imagination.) Now, can you trust this person?

Trust is a funny thing. It has to do with the person we're trusting more than with the thing we're trusting for. When we trust people, it means we know they'll tell the truth, do what's right, keep their word, and come through for us when we need it. We need to know what the person we're trusting is like.

IN GOD WE TRUST

What if it's God standing in the water, waiting to catch you? When we trust in Him, we know we're taken care of because He does all the things that make trust easy. He never lies. He's the only one who always knows what's right and does it. He keeps His promises. He loves us with no strings attached, He's always there and He's completely trustworthy. So, God looks after us and all our needs. What do we do in return? It's simple. We trust Him. Sounds easy, right? Let's take a look.

What does God want us to trust Him for? Oh, everything! Ah-ha! Here's where the rubber meets the road. "Everything" means our money, toys, books, clothes and home, our family and friends, our bikes, skateboards and in-line skates, our schoolwork and chores, our hobbies, talents and abilities, and our past, present and future. All the things we're stewards of, in fact (see pages 8–11). We can trust God with our whole lives, even the tough stuff. No, especially the tough stuff.

THE TRUST TROT

How do we trust? That's a good question. Follow these simple trust steps—learn the steps and start the Trot. *First*, we remind ourselves that God loves us and that we can trust Him. He knows the answers. Our *second* step is to find out what God's answer is. How? We check the Bible! God's written it all down for us. The Bible's the Instruction Manual that tells us how life works best.

Say you've been saving

> **TRIVIA:**
> Before the existence of money, people used to barter or trade goods. If you were a clothmaker or weaver and wanted a bowl, you would give the bowlmaker some cloth. He'd take the cloth and trade you a bowl for it. Later he might trade the cloth to the woodcutter for wood to make more bowls.

May the power of the Holy Spirit fill you with hope. God is in control.

for a while and have $45.00. Your Tithe Tank (see page 20–23) holds $5.00 ready to be taken to church on Sunday and put in the offering plate. Now say you go to the mall one day and see some really cool in-line skates. Their wheels are made using the latest technology and the support they provide is awesome! You look at the price: $50.00. You try them on. They fit like they were made for you! You know you just have to have them. After all, you have $50.00 don't you? You have the $45.00 from your savings plus the $5.00 in your Tithe Tank.

Hold on a minute. The Tithe Tank money isn't yours. It's God's, remember? You've set it aside for Him and His work. But you *really* want the skates. What do you do? Step *one*, you remember God loves you and what He wants you to do is good. Then you do step *two* and check out what the Bible says. *"Honor the Lord with your wealth, with the firstfruits of all your crops; then your barns will be filled to*

overflowing" (Proverbs 3:9-10). It sounds like you better give God His share first. Don't use the $5.00 for yourself. This verse also promises that God will more than take care of you. Trust God by doing things His way. That's step *three*—doing it God's way. You're stepping the steps and doing the Trust Trot.

That brings us to step *four*–trust God to work it out. You use your money the way God wants you to—by tithing, for example. Then you trust God to help you get the other things you might want or need. Leave your desire and the timing for the new skates in God's hands. He'll take care of it. *"May the God of hope*

JOKE:
What would you have if you had 50 pigs and 50 deer?
100 sows *and bucks*.

fill you with all joy and peace as you trust in him, so that you may overflow with hope by the power of the Holy Spirit" (Romans 15:13). You never know. The skates might go on sale!

BIBLE BLANK

Now, there are some things the Bible doesn't cover, such as, should you go to the one- or two-week summer camp? When the Bible doesn't seem to say specifically what to do about a concern, or you're not sure how to act in a situation, don't worry. Be happy. We can pray for help in making the right decision. He cares about us and knows we need His help. We can commit our situation to God, use the wisdom He gives us (or the advice our parents give), follow His principles, and be confident it will work out because we know He'll provide for us.

OUR BIG GOD

How do I know it will work out? Because that's just who God is. He's trustworthy. God is a whole lot bigger than you or me or parents or teachers. . . He sees the whole big picture—the lives of everyone in the world, all interacting and affecting each other. He sees the past, present, and future. He knows each of us inside and out. He knows what's best for us, and He has a plan for our lives. In fact, we could never understand anywhere near as much as God does. So when God says we should save, give, or trust Him for the money we need, we just know that's exactly the best thing to do. And when it looks like things are not going to work out, when it seems the money won't be there when we need it, we don't worry because we know God loves us. We can trust that it's all for our best.

Sometimes God answers our prayers exactly as we want Him to. Sometimes He answers them differently than what we thought would be the best way. And sometimes we can't understand how He's answering them at all. But God sees the big picture, and God loves us. So we know we can trust Him to do what's best for us. That's trust.

Move the "shovel" out from under the heart by rearranging only two toothpicks.

TRUST ISN'T EASY BUT IT'S GOOD

Hey, we never said trust was easy. That's why it's called trust—belief in the honesty, reliability, and justice of another person. We put our trust in the person, not in the thing or event. We can totally trust God because of who He is and because of His love.

Trust the God who knows what is best, who loves us, and works things out for our good when we trust Him. It's simple. We can count on Him. He's guaranteed for life.

TRIVIA:

In Medieval times, the Knights Templars, a military and religious group of knights who fought in the Crusades to get the Holy Land back from the Muslims, stored valuables for people, granted loans, and arranged for transfers of money between countries. This was one of the first banking systems. Banks still do these things today.

Those who trust in the Lord are as steady as a mountain, unmoved by any circumstance.

TREASURE HUNT

MEMORY VERSE

Romans 15:13 — *May the God of hope fill you with all joy and peace as you trust in him, so that you may overflow with hope by the power of the Holy Spirit.*

BIBLE STUDY PASSAGE

1 Kings 17:8–16

⁸Then the word of the LORD came to [Elijah]: ⁹"Go at once to Zarephath of Sidon and stay there. I have commanded a widow in that place to supply you with food." ¹⁰So he went to Zarephath. When he came to the town gate, a widow was there gathering sticks. He called to her and asked, "Would you bring me a little water in a jar so I may have a drink?" ¹¹As she was going to get it, he called, "And bring me, please, a piece of bread." ¹²"As surely as the LORD your God lives," she replied, "I don't have any bread—only a handful of flour in a jar and a little oil in a jug. I am gathering a few sticks to take home and make a meal for myself and my son, that we may eat it—and die."

¹³Elijah said to her, "Don't be afraid. Go home and do as you have said. But first make a small cake of bread for me from what you have and bring it to me, and then make something for yourself and your son. ¹⁴For this is what the LORD, the God of Israel, says: 'The jar of flour will not be used up and the jug of oil will not run dry until the day the LORD gives rain on the land.'" ¹⁵She went away and did as Elijah had told her. So there was food every day for Elijah and for the woman and her family. ¹⁶For the jar of flour was not used up and the jug of oil did not run dry, in keeping with the word of the LORD spoken by Elijah.

This widow really trusted the God of Elijah and look what happened!

1. What difficult thing did Elijah ask the widow to do? (verse 11)

2. Do you think it was easy for her to give up the last of their food? (verse 13)

3. What did God do for her because she chose to trust Him? (verse 16)

What are some things that you need to trust God with? Make a choice today to trust Him. Then watch what He can do for you!

TITHING & GIVING

Larry the Cat

Making a sports or drama team is just the beginning! Once you're on the team, you practice, work hard, play games or perform, and pay fees. Paying fees doesn't *make* you a team member. You pay them *because* you're a member. Being a Christian is like that. Going to church, reading our Bible, and loving God don't make us Christians. Nor does tithing. We do these things *because* we're Christians.

Tithing means we give our firstfruits to God. "Firstfruits" are the first of our resources, including our time, talents, and money. "Tithe" means 10 percent. The way we give it to God is through the church which uses it to help people and tell them about Jesus. God doesn't need our money because He already owns everything. *"The earth is the Lord's, and everything in it"* (Psalm 24:1). We give our money for *our* sakes, to remind ourselves we're God's stewards and everything is His.

The exact amount, 10 percent (a tenth, one dollar for every ten or a penny for every dime), isn't what God focuses on. He wants us to show others that what we have belongs to Him. We do that with our tithe. The important thing is that we give to God first—before doing anything else. Sometimes we think we're too poor to tithe. Wrong! Being poor or rich doesn't change the reason we tithe. We tithe to remind ourselves we're on the team, that we're looking after God's stuff—and to thank Him for providing for us.

Sometimes we think we *only* have to tithe—give 10 percent and no more. Players on sports or drama teams have things to do. Paying the fees and doing nothing else would be silly. Being a Christian's the same. Jesus said, *"Woe to you . . ., because you give God a tenth. . . . but you neglect justice and the love of God. You should have practiced the latter without leaving the former undone"* (Luke 11:42).

So let's be part of the Christian team. Let's show God we know everything's His by giving some back. And let's remember to do the other things God wants, such as obeying Him and loving and helping people.

JOKE:

Was there any money on Noah's ark? Yes, the duck had a bill, and the frog had a greenback.

Larry the Cat

TITHING SUPERHERO

TABBY THE TITHING TIGER HERE

Does tithing scare you? Do you have trouble with math and can't figure out 10 percent? You don't understand why you should give some of your hard-earned dough away like this? You can't see where the money goes anyway? You've never seen God pick it up from the church? Not to worry. Help is on the way! Faster than a speeding calculator. Stronger than a Swiss bank. Able to divide mounds of money into tenths with a simple thought. Is it a superbrain computer? Is it a high-tech digital church interface? Is it a space-shuttle satellite combo? No, it's **Tabby the Tithing Tiger** to your rescue! He's ready to answer all your questions.

You already know what a tithe is, right? You don't really need a superhero to get a handle on tithing and giving, but T. T. T. or, as we call him, 3T, will help out anyway. The Bible calls it "firstfruits." That just means the tithe is the *first* thing we do when we get any money. Take it off the top. It's the cream, the first growth. The best part. It's our first money priority.

All right. Let's take a look at tithes.

GOD'S PICKUP

You read page 19 so you know what tithing's all about. It's us giving back to God some of what He's given to us. Fine. But how do we give to God? Good question. No, God doesn't dive down for a Sunday pickup. We give to His church. The church takes care of it. The church is God's plan. The church isn't the building; it's God's people. They meet together as a group to carry out His plans here on earth, to learn about Him and to grow as Christians. It's how the world learns His fantastic message–the story of what Jesus did for us. It's also God's hand reaching out to help people. All of that takes—you guessed it—money, time, and talents. Where does the church get the resources to do all the things God planned for it? From our tithes!

The people who tithe to a particular church are a part of that church's team. By giving their resources to the church, they're telling people about Jesus, teaching them about God, and helping those who are needy. You didn't know you were doing all that, did you? Now, we don't have to only give 10 percent. We can give more. In fact, the sky's the limit. We can also give to other organizations and people who tell the world about God—like missionaries or ministries that specialize in spreading God's Word.

TRIVIA:

"Dollar" comes from the old German word Daler or Taler. It was a short form of the name of a silver coin used almost 500 years ago. The coin had a picture of St. Joachim on it and was called the Joachimsthaler.

Honor the Lord with your wealth. Give Him the first share.

Fine, you say. Sounds great. But how do I actually do it?

TITHE TANK

Aha, says 3T, you want to know the nitty gritty. Good for you. OK, here's the plan. Divide your piggy bank, or whatever you keep your money in, into parts. Have one part, or maybe one envelope, set aside for tithes. This is your Tithe Tank. Every time you get money—your allowance, pay for a job you did—take one tenth and feed your Tithe Tank.

That means if you get $10.00, you put $1.00 in your Tithe Tank. If you get $7.00, you put $0.70 in the Tithe Tank. Just take the last number off the amount of money you have. If you have $5.55, tithe $0.55. Get the picture? If you get $0.60, you tithe $0.06. That's how you figure a tithe. Simple.

What next? Every Sunday, take the money out of your Tithe Tank and put it in the offering at church. Nothing's easier. The church takes everyone's tithes and puts them in the bank. Then it uses the money to pay the pastors, pay for programs like Sunday school and youth group, and put on special events like the Christmas program, Easter plays, parties in the park, or other outreaches.

REDUCE TO GIVE

Don't forget to keep your eyes and ears open for other places to give. It's great to give to missionaries. Often their

> **JOKE:**
> What kind of a shot do you give a car?
> *A fuel injection.*

whole job is telling people about Jesus. And the only way they get money for food and stuff, and to do their jobs, is from people like you.

But you've emptied your Tithe Tank, so where does the money for giving come from? That's a great question! Giving money comes out of your spending or saving money. Reduce them to give. You take money you would normally spend on yourself or your own wants and give it away so that people can learn that Jesus loves them and died for them. Talk about a great investment! You're giving for people's lives and souls!

What's that? You worked hard for it and have great plans for it? True. But that's the thing, see. It's not yours. It comes from God. He made you able to earn it. Maybe your parents are able to give you an allowance, and He helped them get the money. It's all God's. It's just on loan to you. So if God wants it for His work, you best give it, right? When we give to God's work, God gives back to us. He takes care of our needs. And He gives us more because He knows He can trust us with it.

God says, "Put me to the test" by tithing and giving first. Then see Him bless you.

3T just reminded me we don't only give money. God gave us our talents and time, so we can give our time, energy, and talents to do God's work, too. Say you're a great artist. Give your talent by making posters for church events, to decorate Sunday school classrooms, or to send to people in other parts of the world to cheer them up. Or give a Saturday to help out at the church with cleaning, decorating, or setting up for a special event.

OK. You agree. You're tithing. You're filling and emptying your Tithe Tank. And you're helping God's people spread God's story. Now what?

PARTY TIME

Now you have a party. That's what "tithe" means: Tithe—a Tenth In Thanks to Him for Everything. (Pretty cool how the letters of words can teach you what the word means, huh?) What it means is that tithing is a party—a thanks party. Every time you empty the Tank into the church offering plate you can feel great. And not just because you're being obedient. It's a celebration. It's a reminder that God is taking care of you. He gave you the money you tithed from. He's given you clothes, food, family, friends, talents, gifts and abilities, jobs and allowances, toys and games.

Tithing is a celebration. It's a way of saying, "Wow, God! You're so good to me! You're great at taking care of my needs! And you're generous and kind to me. I'm so glad I can say thanks by giving part of what you gave me back to you! Here it is! Thanks for everything!"

Now you know! 3T is signing off. He's off to rescue another confused wanna-be tither.

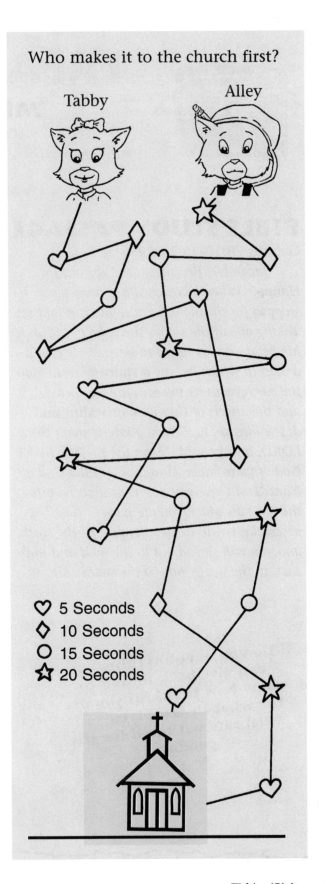

Who makes it to the church first?

Tabby   Alley

♡ 5 Seconds
◇ 10 Seconds
○ 15 Seconds
☆ 20 Seconds

TREASURE HUNT

MEMORY VERSE

Proverbs 3:9,10a — *Honor the LORD with your wealth, with the firstfruits of all your crops; then your barns will be filled to overflowing.*

BIBLE STUDY PASSAGE

Genesis 28:10–15,20–22

¹⁰*Jacob left Beersheba and set out for Haran. ¹¹When he reached a certain place, he stopped for the night because the sun had set. Taking one of the stones there, he put it under his head and lay down to sleep. ¹² He had a dream in which he saw a stairway resting on the earth, with its top reaching to heaven, and the angels of God were ascending and descending on it. ¹³There above it stood the LORD, and he said: "I am the LORD, the God of your father Abraham and the God of Isaac. I will give you and your descendants the land on which you are lying. ¹⁴Your descendants will be like the dust of the earth, and you will spread out to the west and to the east, to the north and to the south. All peoples on earth will be blessed through you and your offspring. ¹⁵I am with you and will watch over you wherever you go, and I will bring you back to this land. I will not leave you until I have done what I have promised you." ²⁰Then Jacob made a vow, saying, "If God will be with me and will watch over me on this journey I am taking and will give me food to eat and clothes to wear ²¹so that I return safely to my father's house, then the LORD will be my God. ²²This stone that I have set up as a pillar will be God's house, and of all that you give me I will give you a tenth."*

We tithe and give to God because He looks after us. He gives us everything we need and promises to bless us with His good gifts when we are faithful to honor Him in our giving.

1. What promise did God give Jacob? (verses 13–15)

2. What did Jacob ask God to do for him? (verses 20,21)

3. What did Jacob promise to give God? (verse 22)

Do you have anything you can give back to God to show how thankful you are for what He has given you? Celebrate with God for His goodness!

BEING CONTENT

Larry the Cat

How many ads have you seen on TV saying you MUST have that toy, those clothes, or that game? Everywhere you look, people are saying you need *things* to make you happy. If you don't have them, they say, you're missing out. They make it hard to be content with what you do have.

The Bible tells a different story. (Check out 1 Timothy 6:6–10.) Paul says all we really *need* is food and clothes. We can be happy with the basics. If we have more, that's great, but, either way, our happiness doesn't come from things but from knowing God is taking care of us. People who love things and money too much fall into a trap that ruins their lives. When you think things will make you happy, you want things. But when you get the things, you find they don't make you happy after all. So you want something

JOKE:

If two shirt collars had a race, which one would win?
Neither, it would end in a tie.

else to make you happy. On and on it goes. It's a trap.

When you're not content:
- you feel sorry for yourself because your friends have things you don't.
- you're jealous.
- you want to get things right now even though you may not be ready for them and can't afford them—these things lead to trouble and make life unhappy.

There's a secret to being content. Learning it takes time. Paul knew that. *"I know what it is to be in need, and I know what it is to have plenty. I have learned the secret of being content in any and every situation"* (Philippians 4:12).

Here's the secret. Contentment doesn't just mean learning to do without things. It's trusting God no matter what situation you're in. It also means being obedient to God and being a good steward of what you do have. Then, if you need more, God will meet all your needs from His wonderful riches (see Philippians 4:19).

God loves you and knows what's best for you. Real happiness comes from trusting Him and being content!

MONSTER ATTACK!!

Nintendo™. Toys. Do-it-all-Dolly. Good friends. In-line skates. Happy family. Outrageous skateboard. Designer jacket. Peace and joy. Funky clothes. Which of these would make you happy? Which do you need to have a great life? Remember, *things* are sure nice, but they don't give us happiness.

COLLECT-IT MONSTER

Down swoops the horrible Collect-it Monster. She has huge claws and a gigantic pocket on her belly like a monstrous kangaroo. She flies into your room and grabs all your clothes, toys, posters, games, books, and furniture. Then she dives into the family room and stuffs the TV and VCR in her pocket. She raids the fridge and gobbles up the cookies, pop, and food. She takes your bike, the family car, all the radios and stereos in the house . . . everything. When she's cleaned you out, she flaps her huge ugly wings and flies away.

There's nothing left. All you have is the clothes on your back and a blanket lying in the middle of your floor!

STUFFLESS BUT CONTENTED

Is it possible to be content with nothing? "NO!" you shout. "I want my teddy bear!" OK, maybe not your teddy, but you'd miss some of your stuff. Can you be happy with what's left? The world around us says we need stuff to make our lives complete. Not true! Life isn't about possessions or money. If our happiness depends on that, it's easy to make us miserable—just take it away. But God didn't make life so that happiness comes from things. In fact, there are millions of people who have only what Collect-it Monster left behind. And many of them are happy.

What do we really need? Food. Clothes. Somewhere to live. And friends and family to love and be loved by. Where do they come from? Ultimately, God! Does God stop taking care of us when we lose our stuff? No way! God takes care of us because He loves us. That will never change. When our happiness is based in God, no one can take it away! We're content and happy because we know God will always make sure we have what we need. And God gives us things to enjoy and look after because He loves us. You may always have nice things. But it's not those things that make you happy.

OK, so we don't need stuff to be happy. We just need to know God's taking care of us. What about the opposite?

DUMP-IT MONSTER

Uh-oh, here comes another monster. This one is already loaded. It's Dump-it

> ### TRIVIA:
> The average 65 year old American who retires after working his or her whole life has a total net worth of $100. That means, if everything was sold and all debts were paid off, all he or she would have left is $100!

Monster! Look out! She's emptying her belly pouch over your house. Down floats more stuff than you've ever seen! Skateboards, supercomputers, games, a huge swimming pool, a room full of the latest clothes, a whole toy store, an ice-cream parlor with flavors galore, a mini motorcycle for the back yard . . . everything you could ever dream of. And it's all yours!

Are you happy? "Yes!" you shout. For how long? Pretty soon you'd get tired of it. Things get scratched and wrecked. You don't have enough space for them. You worry about losing everything again. What if someone breaks in? And besides, a newer model just came out. You have to have it!

No, you don't. You'd soon learn that—surprise!—if you weren't happy without things, you won't be happy with them. In fact, you might be less happy. Things are a big responsibility. They have to be taken care of. Money and

TRIVIA:

About 4000 years ago metal was first used as money. Later, animal-shaped bronze bars were used.

possessions don't give us a good life the way the ads would have us believe.

CONTENTMENT TIME

All right, so what we have—nothing or everything—doesn't make us happy. God does. And knowing that makes it easy to be content. Why? Because we can trust in God's love for us. We know He gave us the ultimate gift—Jesus—so He'll gladly give us everything else that we need (see Romans 8:32).

When should we be content? All the time. That's what contentment is—no

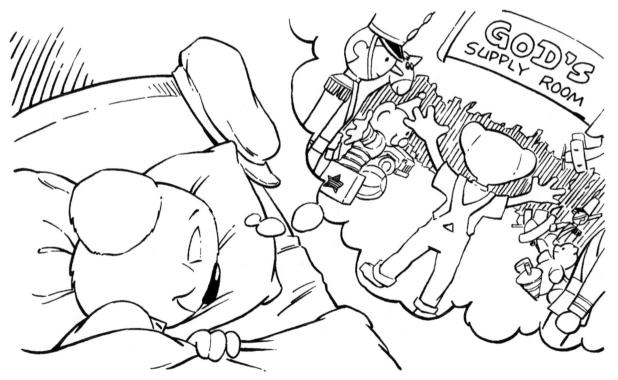

God will meet all your needs with His wonderful riches.

matter what, we rely on God's love for us. We can rest, relax, dump our worries, and trust that God's in charge. The circumstances shouldn't change our contentment because circumstances don't change God. He's always the same. He's always looking after us and giving us what we need. He knows the key to our happiness is trusting in Him, not in things. So when our contentment and happiness come from God, it doesn't matter how much stuff and money we have or don't have. We have God. God has us. And that's more than enough. That's real riches!

RIDDLE:

I know a word with letters three, add two more and fewer there will be. What's the word?

Few

SIMPLE SECRET SOLUTIONS

Sounds simple, right? And it is. Once we truly, truly believe God loves us, it's easy to be content. The world draws us away from that truth with three kinds of temptations. Even Jesus faced them. Here are His secrets for conquering temptation (read Matthew 4:1–11 for the full story).

Temptation #1: Look after yourself—no one else will. Think of yourself first. Fight for your rights.

Secret Solution #1: Obey God. Let Him look after you. Put yourself in His hands and you won't have to fight for yourself. He can take better care of you than you can. He knows you inside and out. He knows what will make you happy. He's getting you ready for the future He has prepared. And what a future!

Temptation #2: Do whatever you want. No one can tell *you* what to do. Make your own rules.

Don't worry about anything. God's peace will watch over you.

Secret Solution #2: Trust God and be happy. Do things His way—it's the best. Some things you want to do, like driving your parents' car, are bad for you. If you did them, you would regret it, hurt people you care about, or hurt yourself. Doing things God's way is the smart way. ***Temptation #3:*** Get what you want. Take what you can get. Things will make you happy.

Secret Solution #3: Don't go after things. Go after the One who made the things. Seek God. When you seek God first, He'll add good things to your life. Trust Him.

When temptation comes, when you start feeling jealous, envious, or unhappy with your life, remember the secret solutions. Also, memorize Scripture verses. Then you can remind yourself what God's way is by saying the verses to yourself. (For good memory verses see the *Treasure Hunt* sections.) When you're anxious or worried about something, remember God's love.

THE PAYOFF

You can be content with God because you know God loves you and only wants what is best for you. He wants you to have a great life. He knows that if you follow His way, you will. God will give us all kinds of things. Having things is not bad. Our attitude toward them is the issue. You see, God tells us to be content because He knows contentment will make us happy. He knows that when we trust Him and, deep inside, know He loves us, we'll have peace and joy. In fact, He promises it in Philippians 4:12–19. God has never broken a promise yet. He never will!

Want a happy life? A life filled with joy and peace? Then live God's way. Trust Him. Learn about His love. Don't get attached to possessions or money. Get attached to God. You won't regret it. Guaranteed.

CONTENTMENT REBUS

A rebus makes a word by combining letters and pictures. These rebuses make things that God gives us. Say the objects out loud to figure out the answers...

TREASURE HUNT

MEMORY VERSE

Philippians 4:12,13 — *I know what it is to be in need, and I know what it is to have plenty. I have learned the secret of being content in any and every situation, whether well fed or hungry, whether living in plenty or in want. I can do everything through him who gives me strength.*

BIBLE STUDY PASSAGE

Philippians 4:6–8,11b–13,19

⁶Do not be anxious about anything, but in everything, by prayer and petition, with thanksgiving, present your requests to God. ⁷And the peace of God, which transcends all understanding, will guard your hearts and your minds in Christ Jesus. ⁸Finally, brothers, whatever is true, whatever is noble, whatever is right, whatever is pure, whatever is lovely, whatever is admirable—if anything is excellent or praiseworthy—think about such things. ¹¹I have learned to be content whatever the circumstances. ¹² I know what it is to be in need, and I know what it is to have plenty. I have learned the secret of being content in any and every situation, whether well fed or hungry, whether living in plenty or in want.

¹³I can do everything through him who gives me strength. ¹⁹And my God will meet all your needs according to his glorious riches in Christ Jesus.

Paul knew what he was saying. He had lived with wealth, and he had lived in poverty. When he wrote this passage he was in prison for his faith. He understood that contentment does not come from things or circumstances.

1. What is the secret to being content? (Hint: Who's in charge? verse 19.)

2. What a cool promise: God's peace will watch over our hearts and minds. What do we have to do to receive that promise?
Don't be _____. By _____ and _____ with _____ present _____ _____ to God.
(verse 6)

3. Thoughts come before actions. What should you be thinking about? (verse 8)

Do you think contentment is a feeling or a choice? Will you choose to be content today? Start by telling God "Thank You" for His gifts to you—your family, friends, home, yourself—your "treasures"!

DILIGENCE/ EXCELLENCE

Larry the Cat

We hear about work all the time. But what is it? It's about who we are, who God made us to be, and how we act that out in our community. Say you love computers and are really good with them. Then working with them is fun. Having the right job's important, but our attitude can make any work fun and important. The right attitude? Diligence and excellence.

"Whatever you do, work at it with all your heart, as working for the Lord, not for men" (Colossians 3:23). This means doing everything with diligence. We're stewards of our work. If God were standing here and asked us to sweep the kitchen floor, would we miss a corner or sweep slowly and lazily? No! We'd do the *Diligence Four-Step:* (1) Work hard. (2) Work well (with excellence). (3) Concentrate on doing the job quickly. (4) Do more than expected. All because we're working for the greatest boss, God!

JOKE:

When was the first tennis match in the Bible?
When Joseph served in Pharaoh's court.

Diligence starts with our heart attitude. In our hearts we *decide* to do our best for God. Then we *do* our best. Pleasing God, knowing He's in charge of our lives—He promotes or demotes us—makes it easier to have a good attitude in tough work situations.

First: We may be doing a job we don't like—think of poor Cinderella before she met Prince Charming. Better yet, take a look at the true story of Joseph. He was a slave, then a prison worker (read Genesis 39–41). If we realize God has us where we are for a good, loving reason, it's easier to work diligently for Him.

Second: We may have to start working for little pay. But remember, we're not merely working for money. We're working for God. He'll promote us and help us get a raise when He knows the time is right. Here's God's *Three Step Work Ethic Plan.*

1. We work hard, with excellence, for God, not people.

2. God rewards our work and blesses it so that people notice.

3. People trust us and give us more to do. Promotion comes from doing things God's way.

Have fun working for the God who loves you. Do it as a service to Him.

DO THE DILIGENCE FOUR-STEP

MISSING: DILIGENCE. REWARD OFFERED!

Great globs of toothpaste! Dollops of dust bunnies! Who was working here? He missed a spot. Several spots. Someone lost his diligence this morning. Mount a search. Call out the troops. Offer a reward.

"Since when," you ask, "is diligence needed for toothpaste and little fuzzies?" Aha! I see your mistake. Diligence isn't just a big job thing. It's an everything-we-do-thing. That's right—from brushing our teeth and wiping out the sink, to homework, ball practice, mowing the lawn, or an executive career—diligence is the key ingredient. If we're doing everything for God, every bit must be done with the Diligence Four-Step. We make our beds the best we can, we wash the dishes and the counter, too. All our chores, homework, and paid jobs are done that way. This means keeping our bedroom so that neither we nor God would be embarrassed if He walked in. Diligence is for every part of our lives.

DILIGENCE FOUR-STEP

Step #1: We work hard. No slacking off. When we're asked to sweep the floor, we get out the broom and dustpan. We clear the floor to get at all the corners. We sweep in an organized way so we won't miss anything.

Step #2. Work well. We don't sluff on the corners or skip bits by sweeping around objects, hoping there's nothing under them. We don't sweep the dirt under the mat. It all goes into the dustpan and is dumped in the garbage with no spills. We do the best job we can.

Step #3. We concentrate and work quickly. We start right away and focus on the job. We don't get distracted, work slowly because we're thinking, or stop to chat. We do the best job in the least time.

Step #4. We do a little extra. We put everything back carefully. We even dust the chairs and tables or wipe the counters. We do something we weren't asked to do.

Sound simple? Sure is. It's extra work, but it's worth it. Diligence is made up of little things: clean the mirror after splashing it, wipe the globs of toothpaste out of the sink, de-sheet the bed on laundry day, and make our homework neat.

CAN YOU TAKE AWAY JUST ONE SHOVEL AND LEAVE EXACTLY THREE SQUARES?

Work at everything you do with all your heart. Always do a little extra.

DILIGENCE PAYS

Diligence is a way to make our time worth more. Then we're paid more. Another way is to get training and education and increase our skills. Then we can do jobs that are worth more and pay more. I don't mean that diligence pays just money. There's more to it than dollars and cents. Diligence makes life easier. It doesn't take much effort to put away a shirt when we take it off. It takes a lot more effort to clean a week's worth of clothes off the floor. Save the big effort by making a little effort now. The satisfaction of a job well done feels great! Doing a good job and having people like it is wonderful.

Diligence is also a character thing. As we're diligent, working for God, our attitude towards people changes. We become people others like working with, looking after, and having as friends. We resemble Jesus.

People notice diligence. It's a looked-for thing. Doing things God's way— trusting He knows what He's talking about — pays off. The Bible says if we're responsible (or diligent) in little things, God will make us responsible for bigger things. He promotes us. He gives us more important things to do because He can trust us. And guess what? People promote us, too. Every boss wants workers with a good work ethic who know the Diligence Four-Step. Four-Step people bring value to their work.

Doing things God's way works out best. You can count on it!

TRIVIA:
Before there were banks and coins, people used to wear their money as jewelry, or keep it in the form of objects they would use every day.

TREASURE HUNT

MEMORY VERSE

Colossians 3:23,24 — *Whatever you do, work at it with all your heart, as working for the Lord, not for men, since you know that you will receive an inheritance from the Lord as a reward. It is the Lord Christ you are serving.*

BIBLE STUDY PASSAGE

Genesis 39:1–6,20b–23

¹*Now Joseph had been taken down to Egypt. Potiphar, an Egyptian who was one of Pharaoh's officials, the captain of the guard, bought him from the Ishmaelites who had taken him there. ²The LORD was with Joseph and he prospered, and he lived in the house of his Egyptian master. ³When his master saw that the LORD was with him and that the LORD gave him success in everything he did, ⁴Joseph found favor in his eyes and became his attendant. Potiphar put him in charge of his household, and he entrusted to his care everything he owned. ⁵ . . . The LORD blessed the household of the Egyptian because of Joseph . . . ⁶So he left in Joseph's care everything he had; with Joseph in charge, he did not concern himself with anything except the food he ate.*

Then Joseph was unfairly thrown into prison. But even there he was diligent.

²⁰ *. . . But while Joseph was there in the prison, ²¹the LORD was with him; he showed him kindness and granted him favor in the eyes of the prison warden. ²²So the warden put Joseph in charge of all those held in the prison, and he was made responsible for all that was done there. ²³The warden paid no attention to anything under Joseph's care, because the LORD was with Joseph and gave him success in whatever he did.*

Because of Joseph's diligence in his work, others were also blessed through him.

1. When you work with diligence, what will be the response of those you are working for? (verse 4)

2. What was Potiphar's response to Joseph's hard work? (verse 6)

3. Working in a prison isn't very glamorous work, even for a prisoner. How was Joseph's performance even in prison? (verse 23)

Do you sometimes sulk and stall about the things you are given to do at home? Can you choose today to "work at everything with your whole heart"? Try it and see how God blesses your diligence!

HONESTY

Larry *the* **Cat**

You've finally made it to the toy store to buy a toy that's on sale. The clerk charges full price! "This is supposed to be on sale," you say.

"Oh, sorry. The sale ended yesterday. That's $6.79."

Sadly, you give her a ten dollar bill. She gives you a five and a couple ones with your change. You walk away trying to figure the change out. She should have only given you ones. You got the toy for half price after all! What a deal! . . . Or is it? What would you do in this situation?

Honesty is a key foundation for our lives. It's so important because it's what God is like. In fact, we know from the Bible that God is Truth. Honesty means always bringing out the whole truth in what we do and say, even admitting things that might get us in trouble. It's not only about truth and not lying or cheating; it's also about making sure we're fair, do our best work, and follow what God has shown us to do. It's being like God.

God's the greatest artist! Artists put themselves—their likes and dislikes, beliefs and way of looking at things—into their paintings. They can't help it. Their art expresses who they are. Everything God made expresses who He is, too. He made the world to work in ways that are like Him. That means that, because God is truth, everything works best with honesty—our relationships, money, words, actions . . . everything. When we choose honesty no matter what, we show that we trust God and want to do things His way. That's a very smart thing to do since His universe works that way, too. *"The integrity of the upright guides them, but the unfaithful are destroyed by their duplicity"* (Proverbs 11:3). It also shows we know God will take care of us. Honesty protects our friendships and makes us trustworthy. It leads to good friends and a good reputation.

So what do you do about being given the wrong change? You return the five dollar bill and enjoy the surprise on the clerk's face. Then you smile your way home!

RIDDLE:

If a jet has a value of one, a plane a value of two, then what value does the Concorde have? *Three, one for each vowel.*

'FESS UP

CRASH!! Did you see that ball pick itself up and fly straight for the neighbor's window? Self-propelled softballs, what an invention! Uh-oh. Here comes Neddy Neighbor. "It wasn't me," you say. "It's this new high-tech ball, see. It looks like an ordinary softball but has this tiny microchip that. . ."

Ever been tempted to respond like that? You begin by trying to get out of it. One lie leads to another until you're buried under a pile of untruths and tall tales. Amazing how people see right through you, isn't it?

Honesty is tough sometimes, but telling the truth at the beginning gets us in less trouble than trying a coverup. People respect folk who tell the truth. Neddy wouldn't have been as angry if you'd just said, "Sorry. I hit a high one. It was an accident. Can I help fix it?"

LITTLE WHITE TRUTHS

What about "little white lies"? "Everyone" tells them. What's wrong with telling a half-truth or fudging on unimportant stuff? The same thing that's wrong with telling big lies. Lies have no size. A lie is a lie is a lie. Can you see God telling a "little white lie"?

Honesty is important for every part of our lives–returning extra change, telling the truth, charging a fair price, doing what we say, working diligently, being on time, doing our own schoolwork, taking responsibility for our actions... Ask yourself a key question, "How would I want to be treated?" Then treat the other person that way.

Honesty isn't something we put on for special occasions like our best clothes. It needs to become part of who we are. We have to decide what kind of person we want to be. Do we want to please God, telling and acting out the truth in everything? Or please ourselves—lying, and being untrustworthy?

HONESTY HINTS

Here are some hints. Take extra change back. Admit you hit the ball. Don't copy

FUNNY BOOKS BY FUNNY AUTHORS

"I Can't Seem to Get Out of Debt"
by Bill Melader

"Dad, I Didn't Do My Chores"
by Miss Ura Lowance

"I Would Really Like
One of Those"
by Willy Save

"I Save a Little All the Time"
by Phil D. Banks

"Be a Smart Shopper"
by Mark Downes
and Luke Forsalles

"Better to Give Than Get"
by Sharon Wittothers

"Giving to Your Church"
by Rich S. Ineven

someone else's homework. Treat everyone equally. Keep your word. Always pay what you owe. If you give something away, it's *gone*! (No taking things back.) Decide to be honest in the little things, and you'll be honest in the big things. You'll become known as a person to be trusted. People will want *you* to do work for them because they know you'll do a good job. God will be pleased with you.

Sometimes we blow it anyway. When we do, we ask God for forgiveness. Then we go to the people we cheated or lied to, put it right, and ask their forgiveness.

HONEST HEART GROWTH

The Bible says, *"I know, my God, that you test the heart and are pleased with integrity"* (1 Chronicles 29:17). If God already knows our hearts, why test them? Sometimes God lets us be tested for our sakes. He knows that every time we make a right choice, it's easier to make the right choice next time. That's how we grow strong in character and become trustworthy.

Jesus said, *"Whoever can be*

TRIVIA:
At first, coins had pictures of gods and goddesses on them. Later, pictures of emperors and rulers were put on the coins. If the emperor was unpopular the coin makers sometimes made his picture unflattering.

trusted with very little can also be trusted with much" (Luke 16:10). When we tell the truth, our conscience lets us feel good. We think of ourselves as honest, and we want to keep being honest. As we continue making the right decisions, we grow into strong, honest people. Then, when a difficult choice comes along, it's easy to keep being honest. People who lie in important things have usually made wrong choices in little things. They haven't grown strong in character. Check out Proverbs for more on honesty. (For example, Proverbs 11:3; 20:17,23; 28:6.)

So 'fess up. Be honest in the itty bitty things. Grow choice by choice to be like Jesus. You'll have a reputation worth trusting.

God rejoices when His people are truthful and fair.

TREASURE HUNT
MEMORY VERSE

Proverbs 11:3 — *The integrity of the upright guides them, but the unfaithful are destroyed by their duplicity.*

BIBLE STUDY PASSAGE

Psalm 112:1–9

¹Praise the Lord. Blessed is the man who fears the LORD, who finds great delight in his commands. ²His children will be mighty in the land; each generation of the upright will be blessed. ³Wealth and riches are in his house, and his righteousness endures forever. ⁴Even in darkness light dawns for the upright, for the gracious and compassionate and righteous man. ⁵Good will come to him who is generous and lends freely, who conducts his affairs with justice. ⁶Surely he will never be shaken; a righteous man will be remembered forever. ⁷He will have no fear of bad news; his heart is steadfast, trusting in the LORD. ⁸His heart is secure, he will have no fear; in the end he will look in triumph on his foes. ⁹He has scattered abroad his gifts to the poor, his righteousness endures forever; his horn will be lifted high in honor. ¹⁰The wicked man will see and be vexed, he will gnash his teeth and waste away; the longings of the wicked will come to nothing.

One way of showing our respect for the Lord is by being honest at all times. This pleases Him very much.

1. God says there are two things we must do to show our honesty. _____ the Lord. _____ in His commands. (verse 1)

2. Have you ever tried to walk around when it is really dark? How can we have God's light to guide our lives? (There are four things.) Be u_____, g_____, c_____, r_____. (verse 4)

3. How long does God say the good things we do will last? (verse 6)

It isn't always easy to be honest, is it? Will you work hard at being honest today, even if it means you might have to pay for something you accidentally broke?

GENEROSITY

Larry the Cat

Flap, flap! Hear that? Generosity Goose flying through—dropping off presents here, food there, furniture on this side, piles of clothes on that, a golden egg over there. How about bikes and skates? Toys to that orphanage. . .

Don't you wish everyone could be well-fed, well-clothed, have nice houses, great toys, good schools, and loving families? But if you've ever watched the news and seen the results of famine, poverty, wars, and earthquakes, you know that's not reality. And there's no Generosity Goose to snap her fingers or lay a golden egg and make things right. Nope, it's our job—you, me and anyone else who has more than just the basics. God gave us the job of giving generously to those without.

Generosity means caring about other people's needs as well as ours. *Needs* are what we must have—basic food, clothes, and a place to live. *Wants* are what we'd like on top of our needs—eating out, new stylish clothes, and a big house. Our *desires* are what we'd *really like* if we could have them—pizza and ice cream every day, gourmet burgers, the latest, greatest designer clothes, our own rooms, a big house with a swimming pool, huge yard and. . . . Know what I mean? Generosity is being willing to give up some of our *wants* and *desires* to help meet others' *needs*. We can do this cheerfully when we remember God owns everything. He'll make sure we're taken care of.

We forget how blessed we are to have the things we do. We need to remind ourselves of the needs of others out there. Think about people who don't have enough to eat, never see a new toy, and/or live in places that are falling apart, without running water, electricity, or even a real bed. Share some of what God has given you with those who have less. That's God's way of taking care of them—through us. It's all God's, anyway. When we're generous with what God gives, He can trust us with even more. *"A generous man will prosper; he who refreshes others will himself be refreshed"* (Proverbs 11:25).

Fluff up your wings, practice a flap or two, and be a Generosity Goose.

JOKE:

Q — What's a motto?
A — *Nothing. What's the motto with you?*

Larry the Cat

GENEROSITY GOOSE, A REAL GIVER

MONEY MOTTO

"Happy with God's gift, plenty or thrift."

THE GIVER SORT

Picture this. A human-shaped Generosity Goose is sorting through her closet, checking her piggy bank, and going through her toy box. She's putting it all in piles, muttering, "One for me, one for you, two for me, one for you, three for me, one for. . . Oops, got carried away." She's buried under piles of stuff. She never realized she had so much! Wait, she's clambering out. Phew! Fresh air!

What is she looking for? Clothes she hasn't worn in a while, toys she doesn't play with, and cash she doesn't need. Why? Because this is the week for Generosity Goose to be a giver and lay the golden egg for others. She'll be taking her old clothes—in good shape, washed and ironed—to her church or the local charity where people in need can get them. She's sending her old toys that still work to an orphanage her parents know of in another country. The kids there rarely get toys. She's going to use her money to sponsor a kid her age in Africa. Then, guess what! She's going to help out in a soup kitchen on Saturday. It'll be lots of work and plenty of fun. And she can talk to people about Jesus. She can't wait!

GIVER HOW-TO

Sound like fun? That is exactly what generosity's about. It involves ourselves, possessions, money and time. God has given us so much. He looks after all our needs and then some. It's easy to give when we know we'll always have enough.

There are lots of places and ways to give to people. Some churches make up baskets at Christmas for poor families, put on special meals, send groups to help in soup kitchens, or sponsor kids overseas. There are lots of organizations that send money and goods to countries that are poor, have awful famines, or are recovering from disasters. Help your parents to find out what groups are the best to donate to.

CAN YOU REARRANGE THESE SIX COINS TO MAKE A CROSS, WITH FOUR COINS ACROSS AND FOUR COINS DOWN?

HOME GOOSE

Don't think generosity is only about giving to people "out there." No way! What good is that if you always grab the last cookie, never share your toys or lunch, and say no whenever your brother or sister asks to borrow something? Generosity starts at home. It starts as an attitude of thanks for God's goodness. Then it's an action. It's holding everything lightly, not hugging it tight in case someone tries to take it. It's being ready to let go and give. Can you handle it? Can you be a real Giving Goose and lay a golden egg for someone?

THE EGG

The Bible says *"Whoever sows sparingly will also reap sparingly, and whoever sows generously will also reap generously"* (2 Corinthians 9:6). If we're stingy, that's how we'll be treated. Giving generously pleases God. And He'll be doubly pleased as He gives generously to us. We can give to others the kind of love God gives to us—generous, kind, and more than enough.

The more we learn to be generous, the more we can remind ourselves how well God looks after us. We can give something away—say money from our savings—and be grateful for God's generosity that we have savings! Many people don't. We can give extra clothes away thanking God that we have extra. After all, some people may only have two dresses or one pair of shorts and a shirt!

Let's take a look in our rooms, closets, and toy boxes to find the golden eggs that God has already given us. Make an omelette and share it around!

TRIVIA:

Coins made in countries where the main religion is Islam never have images on them. The Islamic religion forbids it.

The one who plants a lot will gather a lot. God loves a cheerful giver.

TREASURE HUNT
MEMORY VERSE

Proverbs 11:25,28 — *A generous man will prosper; he who refreshes others will himself be refreshed. Whoever trusts in his riches will fall, but the righteous will thrive like a green leaf.*

BIBLE STUDY PASSAGE

2 Corinthians 9:6–13

⁶*Remember this: Whoever sows sparingly will also reap sparingly, and whoever sows generously will also reap generously. ⁷Each man should give what he has decided in his heart to give, not reluctantly or under compulsion, for God loves a cheerful giver. ⁸And God is able to make all grace abound to you, so that in all things at all times, having all that you need, you will abound in every good work. ⁹As it is written: "He has scattered abroad his gifts to the poor; his righteousness endures forever." ¹⁰Now he who supplies seed to the sower and bread for food will also supply and increase your store of seed and will enlarge the harvest of your righteousness. ¹¹You will be made rich in every way so that you can be generous on every occasion, and through us your generosity will result in thanksgiving to God. ¹²This service that you perform is not only supplying the needs of God's people but is also overflowing in many expressions of thanks to God. ¹³Because of the service by which you have proved yourselves, men will praise God for the obedience that accompanies your confession of the gospel of Christ, and for your generosity in sharing with them and with everyone else.*

God can shower all kinds of blessings and good things on you. God wants our lives to be like a garden in full bloom, sharing His love and goodness to those who come our way.

1. What attitude is important when we give? (Hint: verse 7)

2. Who gives us the resources to be generous and who is responsible for the results of our giving? (Think you can look in the mirror and find the answer there? I don't think so! See verse 10.)

3. How can you cause others to praise God? (verse 13)

What do you get in God's shower? All kinds of blessings. Do you know someone who could use your help today? Be generous with yourself! Share God's shower with those around you.

Larry the Cat

SPENDING

Yikes! Look at that! His pocket's turning black and smoking. Yowch! Fire! Help! It's burning right through his jeans. What is it? Money! It burned a hole right through his pocket! Well, not really. But it sure didn't stay there very long. It left so fast it might as well have burned its way out! He spent it as soon as he got it—on candy. He ate it all, too. Now he's feeling sick.

That's foolish spending. Spending isn't the opposite of saving; it's the opposite of earning. Money is a means of exchange (remember page 32–33?) You exchange your time, effort, and skill for money. Then you exchange your money for things you need. You're spending the reward for your work. Money in, money out. Saving is keeping some of your spending ability for another time instead of letting it burn its way right out of your pocket and into a storekeeper's.

JOKE:

Where does a bird go when it loses its tail?
To the retail store.

Spending isn't wrong and saving right. Saving's just delayed spending. Even giving is spending our money on others. There's nothing wrong with spending. The key is to be wise stewards of *how* we spend. Eventually we spend all our money anyway, so knowing how to spend it is important. There are three general rules:

1. We don't *have* to buy anything. We follow God's wisdom and learn the difference between our needs, wants, and desires (page 39).

2. When we spend, we spend wisely. That means spending it on things God approves of and making sure we get good value for our money—a good product for a good price.

3. We don't spend everything right away. We plan to spend a certain amount and we stick to our plan.

God wants us to trust and obey Him and let Him care for us. Jesus said we can't serve God and money. If we go after money and the things it can buy, we put those things ahead of God. On the other hand, we prove we trust God when we obey Him, follow His principles, and spend wisely.

So trust God and make your spending plan a fire extinguisher!

Larry the Cat

THE SPENDER'S FRIEND

I've tithed, given, and saved. Now I've got my list and my pen for checking things off it. I've got my saved-for-a-purpose money, my spending money and my Spender's Friend fire extinguisher (just in case)—it's a bright red notebook with my spending plan all laid out in it. And I'm wearing comfortable walking shoes. I'm the Totally Equipped Shopper (TES)!

THE LIST

What are TESs' lists like? Well, how old are the TESs? What does their plan say the money's for? What have their parents said they're responsible for? In some families the kids buy their own clothes. In others, they pay for things like library fines or the extra phone line. (When you're older, a big responsibility will be to pay taxes and obey the tax laws.)

Whatever the family lists of responsibilities are, they come first. Responsibilities are *needs*, and needs get paid first. No going to McDonald's with friends until the library fine's paid. The fine's a need. McDonald's is a want or desire.

Once responsibilities are paid for, you move to the next item on the list. That's whatever your plan says you've been saving for—say a new tennis racket. Then comes whatever you want to buy with your spend-on-anything money, like a new book. Ready for a refreshing drink? At the bottom of the list are things you'd like if you can afford them, say a bracelet or comic.

Check items off as you go. (1) Responsibility one: library fine. Paid. Check. (2) Responsibility two: birthday presents. Check and check. (3)

Thoughtful spending has big rewards — not only does our money go farther, our hearts are at peace.

Responsibility three: new jeans. *Check!* (4) Saving goal: tennis racket. *CHECK!* (5) Large slurpy. Check. (6) New book. Cool, I have *just* enough. Shopping's over. We paid our responsibilities, met our savings goal, and had fun with our anything-we-want money.

THE WISE SHOPPER

When shopping, follow the wise buyer's creed: "Shop till you drop but don't spend 'til the end." In other words, look, compare, and gather information. We want to get good products for our money by comparing prices and quality. We look for sales and pray for wisdom and help in finding the best deal. Then, when we've found the best deal, we buy!

SHOPPING GUIDELINES

We followed the plan. We feel good. The plan works because, by following it: (1) We live as stewards of our money, not for what money can buy. (2) Our hearts are safe with God. Our spending shows where they are. "*Where your treasure is, there your heart will be also"* (Matthew 6:21). By following the plan we spend wisely and put important things first. (3) We plan for the future. We sacrifice to get our tennis racket in the future. We build a good reputation by being responsible—and keep our library privileges. We trust God by doing things His way.

THE LOOT

And just look what we're taking home! Our money went further than expected. Getting more for our money is one of the pay-offs for being good stewards. Also, if we keep following the plan, we'll stay out of debt because we won't borrow. If we do, we'll pay it back right away—it'll be in the plan. But the biggest payoff is that the Shopper's Friend— the plan for being good stewards and doing things God's way–keeps our priorities straight. We stay focused on the important things: pleasing God and loving people. We remember to spend our selves, time, and energy wisely. And who stays in charge of our lives? God who loves us. What a plan!

TRIVIA:
The first modern coins were used around 2600 years ago in Lydia (an ancient kingdom that was located in what is now Turkey). They were thick and flat, with images and their value marked on their surfaces.

TREASURE HUNT
MEMORY VERSE

Proverbs 31:16—*She considers a field and buys it; out of her earnings she plants a vineyard.*

BIBLE STUDY PASSAGE

Luke 15:11–24 (Paraphrased)

The Pharisees and teachers of the law were afraid of Jesus because He wasn't like them. He showed love and compassion for the people who needed Him. He told them a story to help them understand. He said, *"There was a man who had two sons. 12The younger one said to his father, 'Father, give me my share of the estate.' So he divided his property between them. 13Not long after that, the younger son got together all he had, [and] set off for a distant country."*

This son wasted his money on foolish things. He did not live according to God's ways. He spent all his money on stuff and then he didn't have any for what he needed. He was so hungry that he even wanted to eat the food he was feeding the pigs. Then he realized that even the servants in his father's house had enough to eat and clothes to wear and a place to live. So he made a decision to return home and ask his father to forgive him. And he did.

The father's response was, *22'Quick! Bring the best robe and put it on him. Put a ring on his finger and sandals on his feet. 23Bring the fattened calf and kill it. Let's have a feast and celebrate. 24For this son of mine was dead and is alive again; he was lost and is found.' So they began to celebrate.*

Unwise spending can cause a lot of hurt. It's better to choose God's way right from the start.

1. We can learn a lot from the people God has put over us. He wants us to honor our parents. Did this son honor his parents by asking for help with his spending plan? (Verse 13)

2. How did the son end up feeding pigs instead of feeding himself? (Do you think he had a spending plan or a spending spree?)

3. Even when we make mistakes, if we see that we are wrong and ask Him to, God forgives us. What did the father do when his son asked to be forgiven? (Verses 22–24)

Asking God for wisdom in our spending is very important. Who else can you ask for help? Would you do that today and start spending according to God's plan for you right now? Don't forget — money is not the only thing you spend. Think about your time and energy and talents!

SAVING & INVESTING

Larry the Cat

In the movie *Mary Poppins* Michael took his money, "tuppence" (two pennies), to his father's bank. The bankers told him to open an account and save all of it. They said it would grow and make him rich. Michael wanted to spend it, so he ran away.

Saving is putting aside a planned amount of our money each month. It helps us get enough to buy things that cost more than we have to spend in one month. It's also a way God helps us get ready for the future He's planned for us—like college, trade school, or university schooling. Sometimes He uses savings to prepare us for unexpected things in the future. And saving gets us ready to help people.

When we save wisely—for a specific purpose such as college, to buy something we need, or to help someone—we're trusting God to look after our future. Saving just so we can have lots of money is foolish saving. That's hoarding. When we hoard, we don't trust God to take care of us. We're trying to take care of ourselves by having lots of money.

Jesus told a story about a rich hoarder who built a big barn to store his wealth in. Then he just enjoyed himself. God called him foolish. He was trusting his money, not God, to take care of him. He died before he could spend his money. What a waste! Jesus told us to keep our riches in heaven. Thieves can't steal them from heaven as they can on earth (see Matthew 6:19–21). God wants us to save wisely, not hoard, and so store up treasure (rewards) in heaven.

The bankers wanted Michael to hoard his money. Michael wanted to spend it all. What should you do with your "tuppence"? You should give to God, keep some to spend, and make a savings plan. You need to decide what you want to save for and put a little bit aside consistently until you have enough. Then you buy what you've been saving for or give the money to people who need it. You'll have treasure in heaven.

JOKE:

Where does a polar bear keep his money?
In a snow bank.

PUT YOUR MONEY WHERE YOUR PLAN IS

Congratulations! You've been putting money away bit by bit for a while. You've been *saving!* What now? Here's a thought: invest it. Investments are ways to save even faster.

WEIGHTLESS INVESTMENT

Psst. Want a hot tip? Give me all your savings, and you'll be rich forever. The breakthrough *null grav locomotor* uses ordinary water (talk about environmentally friendly!) to nullify gravity and make things weightless! Think of the possibilities! Invest here, and you'll be set for life!

If it sounds too good to be true it probably is. Money invested in that scheme becomes weightless, too. It just floats away! Get-rich-quick schemes are poor investments. They're traps (check out 1 Timothy 6:9). Good investing means taking a small, *planned* part of your income and buying something or putting it into an account or business to make more money. When the property becomes worth more, or the business or account makes money, so do you. Investing *wisely* helps your money grow faster. However, poor investing loses your money.

SOLID INVESTMENT

Investing is one of the things people save for. They also save for things they can't afford to buy right away and for the future: summer camp, college, or special purchases such as a car. When we know God is in charge of our future, we know even our savings are His.

God might ask us to use our savings for something else, like helping people in need. Now, **that's** a solid investment—people, not things. We don't need to hang onto "our" money tightly for fear if we don't look after ourselves no one will. Looking after us is God's job! Ours is to be good stewards and be willing to use money the way God wants.

TRIVIA:

The "franc" is the money of France, Monaco, Belgium, Switzerland, Liechtenstein and some African nations. The first franc was a gold coin used 630 years ago (in 1360 A.D.). It was named that because the inscription on it said, "King of the Franks."

LITTLE BY LITTLE

Saving is good. Saving is wise. Saving shows we trust God. But how do we do it? The secret is bit by bit. We budget our money (see page 55–57), and part of our budget is a plan for saving. Every time we get money, we put the amount our budget says into our savings bank and record it in our budget journal. The plan says we're saving for a car, a bike, and summer camp. We record in our journal what we put aside for each

God wants us to think beyond today and what we want.
Wisdom says, "Save for the future."

project. When our journal says we've reached our goal (the amount we decided we'd need) we spend it (for example, we buy the bike). Then we put the money that used to go toward the bike toward our next goal. Little by little!

Also, get your parents to help you find a bank with savings plans for kids. Save your money in the bank and collect interest. That means the bank pays you a bit each month for keeping your money with them. What a deal!

SUCCESS

There are huge paybacks to saving and investing wisely. You don't *pay* interest to someone for borrowing money. You *earn* it instead. While you're saving you can find the best deals. You're ready for the unexpected. You can resist dangerous "deals" that the world throws at you.

The result? Peace and flexibility. No worries about "what ifs." You can change your plan to include helping others because you know everything's under God's control and your needs and wants are taken care of.

So, no *null-grav locomotor* for you. Not unless you check it out and find there really is such a thing that does all they say. A better investment is putting your money into God's kingdom by helping others and being wise stewards. Then you can't go wrong!

TRIVIA:

The first modern banks began in England in 1694.

TREASURE HUNT
MEMORY VERSE

Proverbs 13:11 — *Dishonest money dwindles away, but he who gathers money little by little makes it grow.*

BIBLE STUDY PASSAGE

Genesis 41:15–16, 33–37,56–57; 42:1–2

Do you remember Joseph from when we were talking about diligence? Now look where he is and what he's doing!

¹⁵Pharaoh said to Joseph, "I had a dream, and no one can interpret it. But I have heard it said of you that when you hear a dream you can interpret it." ¹⁶"I cannot do it," Joseph replied to Pharaoh, "but God will give Pharaoh the answer he desires." Then Pharaoh told Joseph his dream and Joseph explained it. He gave Pharaoh a plan. ³³And now let Pharaoh look for a discerning and wise man and put him in charge of the land of Egypt. ³⁴Let Pharaoh appoint commissioners over the land to take a fifth of the harvest of Egypt during the seven years of abundance. ³⁵They should collect all the food of these good years that are coming and store up the grain . . . ³⁶This food should be held in reserve . . . to be used during the seven years of famine that will come upon Egypt, so that the country may not be ruined by the famine." ³⁷The plan seemed good to Pharaoh and all of his officials. [The famine was very bad.] ⁵⁶When the famine had spread over the whole country, Joseph opened the storehouses and sold grain to the Egyptians. ⁵⁷And all the countries came to Egypt to buy grain from Joseph . . . ¹When Jacob [Joseph's father] learned that there was grain in Egypt, he said to his sons,
. . . ²"Go down there and buy some for us, so that we may live and not die."

1. Where did Joseph get his plan for saving for the future? (verse 16)

2. What was God's plan for providing for their future needs? (verse 35)

3. What would have happened to all those people (including his family back in Canaan) if Joseph hadn't been willing to listen to God and obey? (verse 42:2)

God revealed His saving plan to Joseph in a unique way — Pharaoh's dream. Who can you ask to help you find God's saving plan for you? Get started today and watch as God unfolds His plan for you.

Larry the Cat

DEBT & CREDIT

One day you go to the corner store with friends. You realize you don't have enough money to get what you want. Should you go into debt and borrow a dollar from your friend?

Debt happens when you spend money before you have it. With debt, you borrow money to buy something and then start "saving" for it by making payments to the lender. That person charges extra to lend you the money. Instead of putting your money in the bank to earn interest, you're paying interest.

RIDDLE:

A tired weight lifter and someone who spends all of his money foolishly both have the same problem. What is it?

They can't budget (budge it)!

When we save with a plan to buy, God stays in charge. When we go into debt, the lender is in charge. "Buy now, pay later" means spending money we don't have, which God hasn't given us or shown us what to do with. How can we be good stewards if we're running ahead of the Master? It's better for us to learn "delayed gratification"—waiting until we've saved before buying, delaying our pleasure until later.

Credit is different. It's when someone trusts us to buy now and pay them later. If your friend loans you the dollar, she gives you credit. If we have a credit card, the credit card company lets us buy something now (without paying) and sends us a bill.

Wise use of credit is OK. As soon as you go home you should pay your friend the dollar you owe. We should have the money before we buy with a credit card, and always pay the bill as soon as it comes. (Also, it's important to shop wisely for a credit card when you're ready.) If we're smart stewards we can use credit without getting into debt. If we plan our spending, save for the things we want and desire, shop properly, and then buy with a credit card, we'll have the money to pay the bill when it comes. We can use the credit without paying interest charges and without spending money God hasn't given us. If we don't pay it right away, we're in debt to whomever loaned us the money. They'll charge us interest. They're our money boss until we pay them.

So be a credit to God. Don't get yourself into debt.

DON'T SING THE D.E.B.T BLUES

THE D.E.B.T. SONG

Sing the D.E.B.T. song. "**D**oing it my way. **E**verything I want or say. **B**orrow lotsa bucks today. **T**omorrow I won't have to pay. HOORAY! Don't have to pay!"

Hold it! Tomorrow you pay! Debt, borrowing money, doesn't mean free dough. Oh no. In fact, borrowing costs. Remember "interest"? Interest adds to what you borrowed, making the total bigger and harder to pay. Your bubble will burst when your creditors—the people you owe—come collecting. Then you'll sing the real D.E.B.T. blues. "**D**id it my way. **E**verything's gone away. **B**orrowed too much they say. **T**aking it away today."

THE DEBT SLIDE

How do people get in debt? They slide in little by little. They borrow a bit here, a bit there and don't repay. Pretty soon they're in debt for more than they have! Aaagh! They've done the Slide. Now they're singing the blues.

Say you find that special jacket you want. You don't have enough. You borrow $100 from your parents and promise to repay them by the end of the summer. You'll sell oodles at a garage sale, collect cans for the refund, use your allowance, and get a paper route. No problem.

Borrowing now can mean trouble later. Any money we get in the future belongs to our creditors until we've repaid them. While we owe, we can't enjoy our money or use it to buy what we need or want. Borrowing says, "No matter what, I'll pay it back." But the future might not happen as we think. No paper route. No one at the garage sale. The cans only bring in $10.00. The Bible says only the wicked don't pay their debts (Psalm 37:21) and we become slaves of the lender (Proverbs 22:7). Don't be wicked. Pay up. Spend the rest of the summer working off your debt. No burgers, movies, or slurpies. Wash the car. Clean the garage. Mow the lawn. . .

It's important to establish a good "credit rating"—a reputation for paying

PROBLEM:

Jack and Jill both wanted to buy the same bicycle. It cost $100, but neither of them had the money. Jack wanted it right now, so he bought it on the store's credit plan and didn't have to pay it off for one year. At the end of the year he had paid the $100, plus $15 in interest charges.

Jill decided to save her money, *then* buy her bicycle, so she started saving money and depositing it in the bank. While her money was in the bank, it earned her an extra $5 interest. Jill had more time to shop around and she found the same bike for $75.00.

How much more than Jill did Jack end up paying for the same bicycle?

what we owe. Starting with our parents is great training. When we repay them and prove we're trustworthy they'll lend us larger amounts.

AVOIDING THE SLIDE

We get into debt because we want stuff *now!* But we don't need it. We can train ourselves to resist temptation, be content and trust God to care for us.

Three rules to stop the D.E.B.T. blues: (1) Plan for what you want; save, then buy. (2) Don't buy unless you have the money. (3) Pay your creditors right away.

So what would be the best way to buy your jacket? Save until you have enough. Then, if things don't work out, you're not stuck with a big debt, and you're free to do other things with your money. Who knows? The jacket might go on sale.

THE NO-DEBT RIDE

Remember, we can trust God to take care of us. When we don't have the money to buy something we want, God might have something different in mind. If we get it by borrowing, we might miss out on something special. So keep plugged into God's plan for you. Without debt, we're free to follow God. We'll be earning interest, not paying it. (That'll raise a smile!) We'll have a good credit rating and reputation. And we'll be able to be generous and give to others without expecting anything back.

So don't sing the D.E.B.T. blues. Get off the slide and enjoy the No-Debt Ride. It's a thriller!

TRIVIA:

The average family pays $7,000 a year just on interest (the price they pay for borrowing money). If they took that money and invested it every year so they would earn interest instead of paying it, after ten years they would have $150,000!

Be sure to use credit wisely. Pay everything you owe.

TREASURE HUNT
MEMORY VERSE

Psalm 37:21 — *The wicked borrow and do not repay, but the righteous give generously.*

BIBLE STUDY PASSAGE

2 Kings 4:1–7; Romans 13:1,7,8

¹The wife of a man from the company of the prophets cried out to Elisha, "Your servant my husband is dead, and you know that he revered the LORD. But now his creditor is coming to take my two boys as his slaves." ²Elisha replied to her, "How can I help you? Tell me, what do you have in your house?" ... "Nothing at all" she said, "except a little oil." ³Elisha said, "Go around and ask all your neighbors for empty jars. Don't ask for just a few. ⁴Then go inside and shut the door behind you and your sons. Pour oil into all the jars, and as each is filled, put it to one side." ⁵She left him and afterward shut the door behind her and her sons. They brought the jars to her and she kept pouring. ⁶When all the jars were full, she said to her son, "Bring me another one." But he replied, "There is not a jar left." Then the oil stopped flowing. ⁷She went and told the man of God, and he said, "Go, sell the oil and pay your debts. You and your sons can live on what is left."

¹All of you must be willing to obey completely those who rule over you. There are no authorities except the ones God has chosen. Those who now rule have been chosen by God. ⁷Give everyone what you owe him: If you owe taxes, pay taxes; if revenue, then revenue; if respect, then respect; if honor, then honor. ⁸Let no debt remain outstanding, except the continuing debt to love one another, for he who loves his fellow man has fulfilled the law.

Elisha was a prophet of God; he was like a pastor of a church. This woman had a debt that was not her fault. She asked him for wisdom and help.

1. What did Elisha tell her to do? (verses 3,4)

2. I can just imagine that she must have thought this was a pretty strange request. What about her pride? And the jars must have been heavy! What did she do? (verse 5)

3. If you owe something to someone, what should you do? (Romans 13:7)

> God's desire for us is to have only one debt that is never fully repaid. That debt is love. Because His love for us is limitless, He wants our love for others to be limitless. How can you share that love with others today?

BUDGETING

Larry the Cat

"I tot I taw a puddy tat. I did. I did taw a puddy tat." Not just any puddy tat, Tweetie. And not Sylvester. It's Larry the Budget-Master here. No, not "Budgie." "Budget-Master." And I'm a ferocious feline when it comes to the "B" word.

A budget's a plan, a written plan for what to do with money. It's simple. The plan shows how much money's coming in and where it's going—tithes, saving projects, respon-sibilities (clothes, birthday presents, giving . . .) and pleasure spending.

There are two keys:

1. Money coming in has to equal money going out.

If money out is more than money in, you're on the Debt Slide (see page 52–53). If money in is more than money out, you're in good shape. That means you're saving.

2. Follow the plan.

Ask God to help you plan wisely and put your money into the things He wants. (Remember, it's His. We're just—what's that word again?—Stewards!) Once you have your plan, if it says put $5.00 into savings and spend $5.00 on whatever you want, that's what you better do. Say you budget $15.00 a month for the extra phone line your parents put in for you, but you use that money for eating out instead. What happens? The phone goes dead! The company cuts you off. You won't get it back until you pay what you owe. And you'll have to pay the connection fee again.

No. The plan's the key. Your budget will start out simple when you're young and get more complicated as you grow. You might start with three or four categories. By the time you leave home, you could be working with a full 15-category budget. The plan will take care of the details. You just have to follow it. Simple. A little self-control and faith that God's in charge, and it's a piece of cake.

So, Tweetie, take advice from a Cat who knows. Budget.

RIDDLE:

Could you build a house with all four walls facing south? If you could, then what color would a bear be if it walked by?
You could do it, if you built it on the North Pole. The bear would be white, of course…a polar bear.

MAP YOUR BUDGET

LIFE BUDGET: HAVE AMPULE, WILL BUDGET

Professor Mapitout here. I have 36 ampules of energy, 24 of time, and 12 of money. I divide the ampules into each other to find how to spend my energy, time and money. It's simple mathematics: $36 \div 24 \times 12 + 8$ (sleep units) = energy per hour and money per. . . .

Prof. Mapitout's budgeting. We budget our time and energy as well as our money. A certain amount of time and energy is spent on family, chores, school, church, our relationship with God, eating, sleeping and play. If our energy and time budgets get out of whack, we start the Debt Slide. Not enough sleep means no energy for school. No time with God? We get grumpy and behave badly. Without play we get listless. It's all a matter of balance. Map it out and follow the map (the budget).

MAP-IT-OUT

Let's try a time map. First take the must-dos (school, chores), priorities (prayer, Bible study), and no-choices (eat, sleep). Write them down. Fit the should-dos (youth group, homework), want-tos (ball practice), and if-onlys (parachuting) around the musts. Keeping time priorities right makes people around us (like parents, teachers, friends) happy, too.

Budgeting money works the same. We have four categories each with a percentage of our money. Percentage means part of a hundred. Ten percent—10 dollars of a 100. Twenty-five percent—25 of a 100.

Here's the map: *Tithe—10%* (to the church). *Short-term Savings—25%* (Christmas gifts, a new video—things that take several weeks to save for). *Long-term Savings—25%.* There are two sub-categories: *don't touch—10%* (long-long-term things like college, trade or Bible school) and *large goals—15%* (things that take several months to save for, like a bike). *Spending—40%* (For some this will be "free" money to spend how they want. For others this will have sub-categories for responsibilities like clothes, eating out, and phone costs.)

Your budget will grow with you. The goal is to manage your money in a way that pleases God by doing things His way.

Keep track of your budget in a journal

BUDGET BAFFLER:

Put ten toothpicks on a table to make this budget problem in roman numerals. The left side is how much you plan to spend and the right side is how much you have. Obviously you have more budgeted than you have income. Fix your budget without moving the toothpicks...

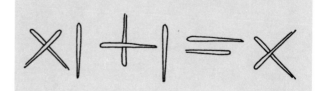

or little red book (remember the Spender's Friend fire extinguisher?) If you don't have a piggy bank with sections, use envelopes. Record things in your journal. When you want to know how much you have toward a saving goal or what you can spend, check the envelope. (It should match your journal.) Take it, and go to it! Don't forget to record what you spend!

(This budget's a suggestion. Make your plan with your parents. The key is to *have* a plan and follow it.)

PAY-OFFS ROLL IN

So you've budgeted your time, energy and money. Now what? You wait for the results to roll in. Being organized in these areas has pay-offs in others. Using your time wisely at school and home helps you use it well at a job. That helps make bosses happy. When you learn to go to God about your money, it'll be natural to ask Him about things like relationships, what to do with your life, who to marry. . . OK, you're not getting married for a while, but you get the point. Your life will have purpose and direction. You'll be in control of how you spend your self, time, and money. You'll accomplish heaps of things because you've learned to plan. You'll have no silly, avoidable money problems. You'll be generous and giving. You'll trust God for your needs and more. Why, the list goes on and on.

The Professor had it right. Plan, pray and map it out and you won't go wrong!

TRIVIA:
In 1993, 28.5 million teenagers in the United States spent $28 billion and persuaded their families to spend another $155 billion!

The wise and diligent man makes good use of every dollar. He has a plan and follows it.

TREASURE HUNT

MEMORY VERSE

Psalm 25:8,9 — *Good and upright is the LORD; therefore he instructs sinners in his ways. He guides the humble in what is right and teaches them his way.*

BIBLE STUDY PASSAGE

Luke 14:28–35

²⁸Suppose one of you wants to build a tower. Will he not first sit down and estimate the cost to see if he has enough money to complete it? ²⁹For if he lays the foundation and is not able to finish it, everyone who sees it will ridicule him, ³⁰saying, 'This fellow began to build and was not able to finish.' ³¹"or suppose a king is about to go to war against another king. Will he not first sit down and consider whether he is able with ten thousand men to oppose the one coming against him with twenty thousand? ³²If he is not able, he will send a delegation while the other is still a long way off and will ask for terms of peace. ³³In the same way, any of you who does not give up everything he has cannot be my disciple. ³⁴"Salt is good, but if it loses its saltiness, how can it be made salty again? ³⁵It is fit neither for the soil nor for the manure pile; it is thrown out. He who has ears to hear, let him hear."

There's an old saying that goes like this: "If you fail to plan, then you plan to fail." This is true not only with your money, but also with your time and energy and abilities.

1. If there is something you believe you should do, what is the first step you should take? (verse 28)

2. What can happen to you if you don't have a plan or budget? (verses 29,30)

3. If we lose track of God's plan for us, then we are like salt that has lost its saltiness. What does Jesus say about its usefulness? (verse 35)

Jesus said that to be His disciple you must give up everything. This doesn't mean you have to give everything away and have nothing. He wants you to understand that everything you have is His for you to use according to His plan, for His purposes. Is there something you need to give to Him today?

PLANNING

Larry the Cat

I have a treasure map here. "X" marks the spot! To find "X" follow the steps: (1) Find the skyscraper 35 stories high with a flag on top. (2) Go two miles directly west. (3) Walk 85 steps north. (4) Turn around twice. (5) Jump four times. (6) Take four hops east. (7) Dig.

Sound complicated? Just take it step by step. The map is your life. The "X" is what God has planned for you to do. The directions tell you how to get there from here. (OK, so it probably won't be walking, jumping, and hopping. But it will still be step by step.) Taking it a step at a time is easy to handle and, with a plan, you'll know it's the right step.

Long-term financial planning means simply drawing a map of where we are and where we want to go. The plan looks at three things: (1) What we believe God has for us. (2) How we'll prepare for that thing. (3) The money needed for the preparation and plan, and how we'll get it. In other words, where we want to go and how we're going to get there. It includes things like schooling, car, house, marriage, family, (sooner or later?) and career.

We never want to make plans that leave God out. We should talk to Him about everything. He loves us and wants the best for us. What we want is to have our financial plan match up with God's plan for us. We plan to make sure we're being good stewards. We need to see if we're doing what we need to do to get where God wants us to go. It's like being in a car and wanting to go somewhere specific. Once we know where we're heading, we check a map to see if the road we're on and the direction we're going will get us there. Remember, though—God doesn't show us everything at once. Our map will need regular prayer and adjusting as we go.

So pray, make your map, and follow it, checking it now and then to make sure you're on course.

RIDDLE:

I can bounce like a ball, but it'll take more than a day. I cost only pennies, but I'm worth what you say. What am I?
A check.

ATTACK YOUR FUTURE

Doctor, Writer, Missionary. Butcher, Baker, Candlestick Maker. The possibilities are endless! Which one's for you?

Remember: (1) God has a plan for you. (2) He's given you gifts and talents that match that plan. (3) He'll guide you as you pray for wisdom. It's a fact. Remember, plan to make your future what God wants.

PLAN OF ATTACK

Pray about what God wants you to do when you grow up. Ask your parents to find people (maybe at church) with that job. Talk to them. What do they do? What training and grades do you need? Get advice from parents, pastors, or school counselors. Figure out training costs. Your budget's *long-term "don't touch" savings* is for this. Set your goal.

Keep a page in your budget journal for careers you're exploring. List schools you could attend with their entrance requirements. Get volunteer experience. What summer jobs will prepare you? (A good resource is MMK's "*50 Money Making Ideas for Kids*" published by *Thomas Nelson*.)

Stay flexible. As you grow, God may put something different in your heart. Transfer what you've been saving to your new goal. If your savings won't be enough, put more toward it. Get a job. You could apply for scholarships.

Remember the treasure map—one step at a time. The key is to give yourself to God and follow Him. Your parents, teachers, and others can help at each step with what's next.

Following a plan means a smoother ride toward your "X"—God's great plan for your life. God's plan takes into account your likes, talents, abilities, what's good for you and what you're good at.

Follow God's map to the real treasure—a lifetime of doing what you were made to do!

God wants us to plan. Our goal is to follow Him so the final outcome will be His plan.

TREASURE HUNT

MEMORY VERSE

Proverbs 21:5,21 — *The plans of the diligent lead to profit as surely as haste leads to poverty. He who pursues righteousness and love finds life, prosperity and honor.*

BIBLE STUDY PASSAGE

1 Chronicles 28:9–12; 29:14,18,19

⁹*"And you, my son Solomon, acknowledge the God of your father, and serve him with wholehearted devotion and with a willing mind, for the LORD searches every heart and understands every motive behind the thoughts. If you seek him, he will be found by you; but if you forsake him, he will reject you forever.* ¹⁰*Consider now, for the LORD has chosen you to build a temple as a sanctuary. Be strong and do the work."* ¹¹*Then David gave his son Solomon the plans . . .* ¹² *He gave him the plans of all that the Spirit had put in his mind for . . . the temple . . .*

There were plans for all the rooms in the temple. Many people gave different things to fulfill the plan.

Then David began praising God. ¹⁴*"But who am I, and who are my people, that we should be able to give as generously as this? Everything comes from you, and we have given you only what comes from your hand.* ¹⁸*O LORD, . . . keep this desire in the hearts of your people forever, and keep their hearts loyal to you.* ¹⁹*And give my son Solomon the wholehearted devotion to keep your commands, requirements and decrees and to do everything to build the palatial structure for which I have provided."*

David received a plan for the temple from God and passed that plan on to Solomon for Solomon to complete. God has a plan for you, too, and it is just as complete.

1. David understood that the "why" of our planning was most important. Where did he tell Solomon to keep his focus? (verse 9)

2. What two things did David tell Solomon to do with the plan? Be _____ and _____ _____ _____. (verse 10)

3. Your heart is the key to your actions. To whom should your heart be true? (verse 18)

Just as God chose Solomon to build His temple, He has chosen you for a special purpose, too. It is always an adventure to walk in His footsteps! Will you commit yourself to His plan for your life today?

Larry *the Cat*

CONCLUSION

TOP CATS CLUB

You made it! What a ride! Look at your accomplishments! You've learned God's House Rules for Stewards, mastered the Trust Trot and Diligence Four-Step, met superheros and monsters, seen that little white truths are better than lies, found the golden egg in your closet, designed a little red fire extinguisher for pocket fires, avoided singing the D.E.B.T. blues, conquered the Debt Slide, mapped your budget, planned your future, hunted for treasure, and memorized verses!

Phew! You've done it all. So it's time to be inducted into the exclusive **TOP CATS CLUB**. Welcome and Congratulations! You are now a Totally Obedient, Prepared, Content, And Trusting Steward, a Child Living Under a Budget.

This exclusive club is for kids who choose God's way! TOP CATS believe and/or do the following:

(1) God's in charge. He loves us and knows how things work best, so everything He tells us to do is for our good, because He wants to give us a great life.

(2) Everything is God's. He's given it to us to use and look after. Since it's all His, we can be generous to others. When we do it His way He looks after us and gives us everything we need to enjoy life.

(3) We agree to give back to God some of what He gives to us and use His money how and when He wants.

(4) Money isn't everything. We know the difference between wants, needs, and desires. We're willing to put others' needs ahead of our wants and desires.

(5) We do the Diligence Four-Step. We work hard, well, fast, and do a little extra.

(6) Truth is tops with Top Cats. Lies are out. There are no such things as little dishonesties—one size fits all.

(7) We use our money wisely, spend according to our budget, and follow the plan.

(8) We save; we don't hoard. We pay our bills and don't get into debt.

(9) We plan our future with God, map it out in prayer, and follow it one step at a time!

Sound like a lot? Not really. The key is "little by little, choice by choice." Making the right choices in small things means big things will take care of themselves.

Remember that God wants us to enjoy everything He gives us! So, focus on Him and truly enjoy being a Top Cat. You'll have a great life... guaranteed!

TRIVIA: Abraham was considered very rich because he had lots of cattle as well as silver and gold.

Money Matters for Kids™
Teaching Kids to Manage God's Gifts

Lauree and Allen Burkett are the co-founders of **Money Matters for Kids™**. God has planted in their hearts the commitment to see the next generation grounded in God's Word and living His principles. The vision of **Money Matters for Kids™** is to provide children and teens with the tools they need to understand the Biblical principles of stewardship and to encourage them to live by those principles.

Visit our Web site at: **www.mmforkids.org.** We welcome your comments and suggestions.

Money Matters for Kids
Lynden, Washington 98264–9760

building Christian faith in families

Lightwave Publishing is a recognized leader in developing quality resources that encourage, assist, and equip parents to build Christian faith in their families.

Lightwave Publishing also has a fun kids' Web site and an internet-based newsletter called *Tips & Tools for Spiritual Parenting*. This newsletter helps parents with issues such as answering their children's questions, helping make church more exciting, teaching children how to pray, and much more.

For more information, visit Lightwave's Web site at: **www.lightwavepublishing.com**

Lightwave Publishing Inc.
133
800–5th Ave.,
Suite 101,
Seattle, WA
98104–3191

or in Canada:

Lightwave Publishing Inc.
Box 160
Maple Ridge, B.C.
Canada V2X 7G1

A MINISTRY OF MOODY BIBLE INSTITUTE

Moody Press, a ministry of Moody Bible Institute, is designed for education, evangelization, and edification. If we may assist you in knowing more about Christ and the Christian life, please write us without obligation:

Moody Press, c/o MLM
Chicago, Illinois
60610

Or visit us at Moody's Web site: **www.moodypress.org**

ANSWERS

THE TREASURES ARE FOUND IN:
Ephesians 6:10–18 — the armor of God:
Belt of truth — Trusting God
Armor of godliness — Diligence/Excellence
Shoes of good news — Honesty
Shield of faith — Long-term Planning
Helmet of salvation — Saving/Investing
Sword of God's Word — Contentment

Galatians 5:22–26 — the fruit of the Spirit:
Patience, Love — Spending
Kindness, Peace — Generosity
Goodness, Joy — Debt/Credit
Faithfulness — Stewardship
Gentleness — Budgeting
Self-control — Tithing/Giving

Pg. 29 - Rebus
Family, ice-cream, friend, toys, school.

Pg. 52 - Jack & Jill
Jack had to save up $115, and Jill only had to save up $70, Jack paid $35 more for his bicycle than Jill.

Pg. 56 - Budget Baffler
Look at your question upside down.

Pg. 10

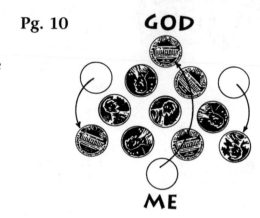

Pg. 32

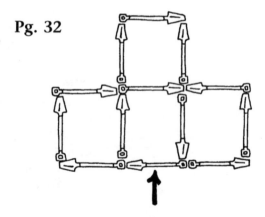

Pg. 40

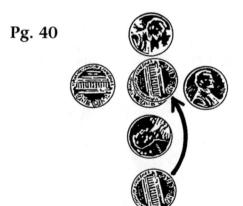